loved
loving
love

written and illustrated by
corin filmer

ISBN:978-1-7330931-2-5

acknowledgments

my heart is filled with gratitude.

alan, my husband for his can do attitude, love, patience and support.

eliane, chloe and ryan, my children who have read, listened to and given love and assistance.

david my father who encouraged me to share my poems.

roberta kautz who first called me a poet.

sheri cleary who has inspired, challenged, and emboldened me to confront my fears and grow my faith.

the wwtw sisters who have listened, suported, given ideas, feedback and most importantly friendship.

martha sandino for her infectious enthusiasm and helping me get this book to the finish line.

sisters at vbc: gwen barnett who loves me day in and day out. fritzeen scott who encouraged me to read the key poem at my baptism, connie johnson for graciously proof reading my book.

ronda edmondson for giving me the key.

most importantly God, because without God i would not have been able to do any of this.

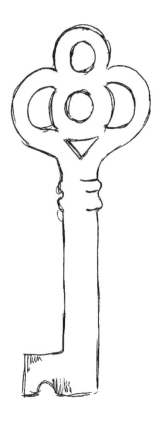

about the key

sitting at my kitchen table clutching a
key in my hand. not sure why but
feeling it was what I should do.

it was an old key, a simple key, its
origin unknown. i had recently chosen
it from a group of keys on a table.

i had been attending a church for a
while. capo beach calvary was my first
experience of church in america. It was
in an old bowling alley, had a modern
worship band, and was NOTHING like any
church i had been to before. full of
openly broken people. i would go alone,
sit by myself and often cry in the
dark... but return week after week...

so to the key in my hand. i had decided
to do a bible study (another step into
the unknown). a group of smiling ladies
welcomed me to their table, on which
sat an old rusty door lock surrounded
by keys. at the end of the study, the
group leader, explained how the keys
represented Jesus and the old lock our
hearts. she invited each of us to
choose a key to keep.

this was the key in my hand. the one i
couldn't put down. i opened my bible to
begin... so many questions in my heart.

i reached for a pen and began to write
"the key."

about me

there i was. on the bathroom floor,
curled up, with my knees close to my
chest, sobbing. sobbing in exhaustion.
sobbing uncontrollably. sobbing as
though i might not be able to stop.
sobbing because there was nothing else
i could do.

eight months previously my husband, our
three young children (all under the age
of four), and i arrived in a small
country inn in massachusetts. we had
just moved into a room with two queen
beds almost touching and a small
sitting room. this was going to be our
home for the next month while my
husband was working on the development
of a micro-chip.

so one month became two, and autumn
days came. halloween arrived and with
it the first snow. winter set in and
the thrill of playing in the deep
powder snow wore thin. as the months
passed, the problems at work led my
husband's health to deteriorate. he
would return home stressed and drained.
i was exhausted and beginning to feel i
could no longer keep everything
going...

and so, one day, while my children were
napping, i went into the bathroom and
closed the door. the feeling of
loneliness and helplessness was
overwhelming. i had no family, no
friends, no support at hand. i could

not go on. who else was there to turn
to? i sank to the floor weeping, and in
my isolation and desperation all my "i
can manage," all my "i can do this,"
came crashing down. in that moment of
feeling totally alone and helpless, i
cried out to God for help. there was
no angel, no blinding light, BUT there
was a peace. it was in that tiny
bathroom; it was in my heart at that
moment of need. my sobbing stopped, and
i felt a sense of peace that surpassed
my understanding. i had for the first
time in my life acknowledged God. I
acknowledged Him and He loved me, as He
always had. i felt His total and
complete love, and i knew that i was
not alone.

a few weeks later we found ourselves
back in our home in france. i had a
constant thought in the back of my
mind. i acknowledged God. what do I do
now? what happens next?

a few weeks later my husband got a call
from a startup company in southern
california, and six weeks after that i
was sitting in another hotel room
waiting to move into our new home. it
seemed that every person i met would
ask, "where do you go to church?" so
when a neighbor invited me to her
church, saying, "you will like my
church; we meet in an old bowling
alley," i went along rather nervously.

looking back I smile at how God found
the perfect place for my faith journey
to begin.

contents

acknowledgments iii

about "the key" v

about me vi

1   the key 11

2   the path 13

3   togetherness 15

4   worship 17

5   good Friday 19

6   worship 2 21

7   fellowship 23

8   touch 25

9   one 27

10 where i find myself 29

11 believe 31

12 beautiful 33

13 from behind the curtain 35

14 grief 37

15 patience 39

16 hold me 41

17 open me 42

18 teach me 45

19 i am loved 47

20 in Your hands 49

21 come to me 51

22 my heart in Yours 53

23 faith 55

24 open hands 57

25 a gift 59

26 one step 61

27 rest in Me 63

28 separation 65

29 Your peace in my heart 66

30 dance with Me 68

31 remember Me 71

32 baptism 73

about you 75

the key

i close my eyes
and see
more clearly
than i have for years

this key
more ancient than the heavens
calls my name
as it has always done

only now
does it reach my ear

only now
do i reach to touch
its perfect trinity

come open me

the path

life is sharp
and so many times
it pricks unmercifully

i search
eyes open
yet in blindness
believing i can find the path

yet my efforts fail me

the more i think, calculate analyze
the more i hit
frustration

again and again,
so stubborn the self
... if i think more
      ... in greater abstractions
            ... and tangents
i shall find the way

again and again
the path's simplicity eludes me

and it is only once i dare to yield
and with quiet confidence in You
relinquish control

i close my eyes
and leave the tangles of my mind
and the path finds me

togetherness

round and smooth
such perfect lines and
individual beauty

carefully placed
on a path
did we forget?

aimless movement
in an imperfect world

alone in the crowd

and then...
a flame touches our spirit
and once alight
emboldened passion glows

almost imperceptible at first
and change...
takes place

then
our hearts ablaze,
a softening of edges
blurs the "us and them"

and slowly...
a new shape appears

where strength is found
in love and understanding
and togetherness

worship

swaying to the music
clapping
singing
hands raised
hearts open

one voice...
echoed by many

words of praise
on my lips
once brought tears
and sorrow

how could i have left You
outside of my life?

and now there's forgiveness
a joy in reunion

so many single voices
unite to stir my soul

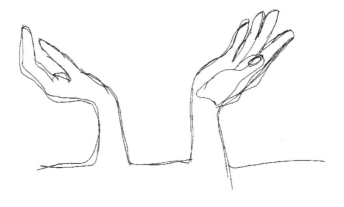

good friday

this day of passion
like none before or since

filled with such pain
and hatred
lies, deceit

so many sins for just one day to bear

and yet its name is good

for on this day
a sacrifice so pure
gave
grace forgiveness mercy
to us all

and at what cost...
and so...
in white linen with majesty we may be

for on this day
love triumphed on calvary

worship 2

eyes closed
waiting for You
nervous of baring... my soul...

then
gradually...
emboldened

words on my tongue
rhythm in my mind
hands turn
to You

and i feel
a presence
an invitation
to come

and as i reach
to touch You
i see a child
arms outstretched
laughing and running
joy on my lips
and tears on my cheeks
when i realize
that child
is me

and what i feel
is my contentment
in Your love

fellowship

at first is a cross
where light and warmth
call to our restless hearts

come and sit
spend some time...
with Me

share...
your needs and problems
your cares and tears

and I will hear
    I will hear
you are not alone

and as we sit
and share
we feel the warmth within

and...
together...
slowly...
the edges blur

we touch and are touched
and find strength
in our togetherness
in His love

and we hear
    we hear
and we are not alone

touch

i close my eyes
and choose to focus
elsewhere

is it retreat?
a move to safer ground
away inside?

but i am not alone

i sense Him
welcoming me
patiently waiting
did it really take this long?

forgiveness and love

no words are spoken
a hand extended
a silent touch
that physical need...
is it just mine?

such joy warmth and healing
i know is shared

and time stands still
for a moment
and in that simple touch
i have all i need

one

one love
so central to our lives
burns with a blazing passion

it calls us to come and gather round
come close and share the warmth
within

and gradually...
a flow so pure
bursts forth
and drenches all who have come near
and in turn
we melt and mold
form new bonds
face new boundaries

and where our love may fail
so the greater love pours forth
and makes us whole

and our hearts become one

where i find myself

am i waiting to go forward?
or trying to stay back?
what is this place of timelessness?
where i find myself?

where i truly find myself...

in the waiting
and the stopping

there is time...

  to pause
    and ask
       and listen
           and maybe even hear

the wisdom of peace
the calmness in a breath
the rhythm of my heart beating

a moment lost in You

believe

where did your journey start?
do you remember?
that first step...
so small and weak
it seemed

yet
life changed

step by step
taking hold of our fear
and letting go
truly letting go
to follow the water
on its path

do you have the courage to keep in the
flow?
so many things slow us down
and side tracked
time passes us by

yet the path is always there
calling to us
and if we choose to hear
the gift of courage
gives us strength
to take that leap of faith
and believe

beautiful

in wild fields
o'er rolling hills
colors blur
in the wind's caress
breathtaking beauty
with a careless precision
each one's
unique character
reveals such love in the detail

yet together
that beauty magnifies
the contrasts
and shadows
the shapes
and movement
makes a bouquet for the senses
that overwhelms

eyes close
in gratitude and awe
i breathe deeply
and realize
that i too am that beauty
bathed in Your love

from behind the curtain

it's time
long time
to listen
and believe
what You've always said
in my heart
it's all You

belief
is the key
no need to hide
to feed the fear
and insecurities
of the world
it's time
to go beyond
and shine
Your light

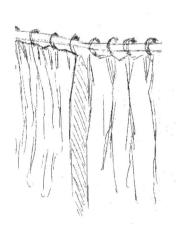

grief

overwhelmed
and scared
to share
the abyss within
it is a lonely
        narrow
              solitary place
deafened by silence
i struggle on
blinded
alone
too dark
to stay
too long

though
in Your presence
the tears can flow
pouring from my heart
                    my mind
                         my soul

pouring
pouring
is there no end?

fill me with Your light
                    Your truth
                         Your hope

let them guide me
in faith
and remember
always

Your love

patience

thank you
for Your patience
daily

another sin
another weakness
forgiven
in grace
and mercy

open my heart
to share
this gift
this patience
daily

of another's sin
another's weakness
forgiven
and forgotten
again
and
again
in mercy
and grace

hold me

hold
hold me
close

closer than i've ever dared

safe
so safe
surround me
calm me

take
take all my pain

give
give love more than i've ever felt

stay
stay always with me

share
share more than i've ever known

hold
hold me
close

open me

tightly
we hide
closed
in our sanctuary

or so it seems

shutting out
and shutting in
drowning in our solitude
too scared
to let
You close

yet
knowing
we can't continue
in the dark
alone
so...

open me

let there be light
on my face
a glow
a peace
a call
to open
again
slowly

open me

to feel the warmth
touch my heart
and melt the sadness

open me

to Your voice
Your work
Your plan
Your love

teach me

You come down
here to me
where i am
with what i need
to learn

show me gently
with such patience
take Your time
to show me how
to hear

time and time
no rush to finish
open up
my eyes
to see

all with love
so You encourage
every step
i'm scared
to make

teach me
teach me
gentle teacher
so my heart
knows how
to love

i am loved

i am loved
 beyond secure
i am loved
 beyond belief
i am loved
 and accepted

rebellious as i am

i am loved
 and forgiven
i am loved
 and redeemed
i am loved
 and adopted

chosen as i am

i am loved
 in grace
i am loved
 in faith
i am loved
 in truth

blessed as i am

in Your hands

held
cherished
secure
in Your hands
safe
such freedom
in Your firm embrace

a moment of silence
a brief time
to share
no need for words
to break
our togetherness

then gently
expertly
the love flows
from You
the song begins

where will it lead us?
whose life will You touch?
how will You choose
to reach
each heart?

who knows
the contortions of Your plans and
dreams?
all You ask of me
is to follow
Your lead
Your grace
Your rhythm
willingly

come to Me

come to me and rest
in truth and love

bring your brokenness
your imperfections
your fears and insecurities
and share your pain
spend time with Me
quiet and still

know you are Mine
and open your heart

dare to trust
and be real
and lose yourself

laugh with no fear of tomorrow
bring Me your today
leave yesterday behind

in honesty
feel the rhythm of grace
and stay
a while

my heart in Yours

loved
loving
love

feeling
my heart in Yours

lifted on wings
to a place of peace
filled to overflowing
with a sense of joy
You know me
and love me
still

my heart in Yours
feeling

love
loving
loved

faith

Your face
Your smile
Your eyes
Your voice

one i've never seen
never heard
never felt

wanting
desperately
something to hold
to feel
to touch

but

You are not
of this world
and i must learn
to try and understand Yours
and believe

open hands open heart

hands and heart
open
searching another's...

vulnerable
lonely
though not alone

empty inside
needing
a hand to hold

in that moment
You come
take my hands
like a father takes his child's

i feel

safe
secure
calm
at peace

loved

a gift

a gift
we didn't earn
is freely given

what shall we do with it?

it is beautiful to look at
hard to grasp
engaging to consider
awesome to behold

but what to do with it?

keep it safe?
locked away?
to observe
when we feel the need?

keep it at a distance?
too much to really fathom
how did we deserve it?
how can we repay it?

keep it hidden?
lest it should change our lives?
upset the comfort
break down the walls?

the answer is simple...

share it
live it
love it

one step

one step
today
here and now

one step
in faith
trust
obey

one step
in love
calm in the storm

trusting in You
for
one step
more

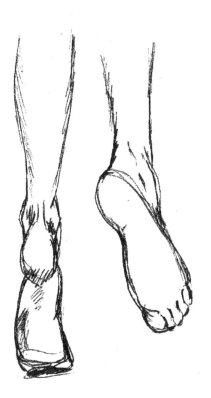

rest in Me

be still and know
that you are loved

have confidence in that love

I am constant
forgiving
loving

let Me into the darkest parts of your
heart
to your hurts and fears
let us rest there
     together
         quietly

feel safe
as My light slowly touches and warms
those places
         you have hidden
                 for so long

there's a sense
of peace
and healing
as My arms
enfold you

in your heartache
in this moment
in our embrace

feel My love
and
be Mine

separation

feeling adrift
cut off
alone

yesterday's failures
overwhelm
drowning in my guilt

early morning calls
to tease and taunt
relentlessly
accused of future insufficiencies

so this is where i am?
this is separation?

help me find You in today

take my hand
in the now
renew me
in the present
lead me in Your will

take my fears
use my weakness
guide me on the path
You have prepared
for me

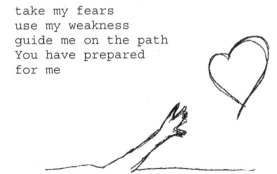

Your peace in my heart

when i rest
in Your arms
so safe
i never want to leave

times...
when a peace
fills my heart
a calm
a tranquility like
nowhere else
    nothing else
        no-one else

yet...

there are days
when a fear grips my heart
so strong...
i barely dare to breathe
such panic rules
and life is
just survival

why do i let it in?
to spread and fill until
it grips my soul?

help me
to turn to You
each day

to lean on You
and trust You
to listen
when You call
my name...
and tell me
You love me

let that love
bring Your peace
to my heart...
always

dance with Me

if I held out My hand
would you take it?
if I called out your name
would you come?

come dance with Me?

would you take that step
and join Me?
where you are
who you are
what you've seen?

come dance with Me?

brave enough
to trust Me
when I say
I see your heart and love you still?

come dance with Me

I would hold you
so close
I would lead
and you would choose to follow

come dance with Me

and you would know
peace
in the dance
with Me by your side

come dance with Me

come
feel the rhythm
know the beauty
give Me your hand
your heart
your life
and... dance!

remember Me

hold Me close
like a precious jewel
My brilliance
reflecting
refracting
endlessly
flawlessly

remember Me

feel My strength in your life
the warmth in your heart
the hope and the joy
the salt and the light

remember Me

keep Me with you always
turn to Me in trouble
gaze on Me
never tire of discovering My mystery

remember Me

share My stories lovingly
of mercy
wisdom
truth

know I am with you
even when the world distracts

remember Me

I am patiently waiting
and always
remember you

baptism

a step
into obedience
into love
into joy
into a living mystery
older than days

into a future
where courage
meets clarity
and conquers fear

in a gasp for life
a new heart shift
where tears flow
and doubt meets trust
and i focus on
the cross
and embrace a greater freedom
in Him

about you

God loves you

this might be the first time you have
heard this. like me you have lived
life with no thought of God, His
love, or your need for that love. i
urge you to take a moment to reflect
on this love. re-read a poem that
touched your heart and let it be
opened....

visit my facebook page "the key
designs" for a link to my facebook
group "loved loving love" or my
Instagram @thekeydesigns share your
thoughts, your favorite poem, your
journaling with me and others.

how is Jesus calling you?

for God so **loved** the world that he
gave his one and only Son, that
whoever believes in him shall not
perish but have eternal life. for God
did not send his Son into the world
to condemn the world, but to save the
world through Him

john 3:16-17

Made in USA - Kendallville, IN
1137251_9781733093125
10.14.2020 1332